Remembrance

A Journal of Awakening and Self-Renewal

Carolyn M. McKanders

Copyright © 2007, 2009 Carolyn M. McKanders
Remembrance: A Journal of Awakening and Self-Renewal

All rights reserved. No part of this publication may be reproduced, stored in a retrieval system, or transmitted in any form or by any means – electronic, mechanical, photocopy, recording, or any other – except for brief quotations in printed reviews, without the prior permission of the publisher.

ISBN 13: 978-1-933972-18-3
ISBN 10: 1-933972-18-1

Cover and interior design by Christina Dixon

Printed in the United States of America

~Dedication~

With gratitude and love
To my husband Ken and to our children - Kimberly, Karla, Kristal and Kenny - divine reflections who teach me every day.

~Special Acknowledgements~

I acknowledge God, the Source within all.
And...I am filled with gratitude for the editing work and loving support given to me by Carole Evans and Robin Render.

~ Preface ~

This journal is offered as a gift, intended to "nudge" each of us into a deeper understanding of who we are. I invite all of you who use this journal to allow the reflections that are prompted by its pages to move you into the magnificence of love and grace that is always who you are... your true identity.

Imagine a beggar who is unknowingly sitting on a treasure chest; he keeps holding out his cup and hoping for coins and handouts. If only he would shift his position, stand up and look inside, he would have more than his wildest dreams. With that image in mind, I invite you to shift your viewpoint, look inside, and remember that you are already the treasure and the blessing and the Divine.

Allow the words and phrases in this journal to serve as a "starting point" from which you move inward... a catalyst that stirs the soul and awakens insights. Then listen, notice the messages, accept the flow of grace, and journal the magic in whatever way speaks to you. Some ideas divinely resurfaced throughout the journal and I have deliberately left them in as they appeared.

Just like the flowers and trees, we are perfect as we are; it is only illusion and our confusion that separates us from our wholeness: *God within. Use this tool to refocus and to remember the embodiment of who you really are.

God is, You are.

Remember...

> "Whoever deeply searches out the truth
> will not be deceived by paths untrue,
> Shall turn unto himself his inward gaze,
> Shall bring his wandering thoughts in circle home
> And teach his heart that what it seeks abroad,
> It holds in its own treasure chests within."
> Boethius, A.C. 480- 524

* For the purpose of this journal I ask that you move beyond the words used to identify the source of life. Whether the word you use is God, Allah, Spirit, Source, Beingness, Truth, Love, Tao, Light, She, He or something else, know that our meanings are the same.

~ Using Your Journal ~

The words and phrases in this journal are intended to stir introspection and self-reflection. Move far past them - using them only as signposts pointing the way inward. Stay in "feeling" and allow yourself to go where the feelings take you. Then capture and record those images and "ahas" in words and pictures. Return to these pages often and use them to enhance your awareness and to monitor your progress as you walk your spiritual human path to higher levels of consciousness.

I Remember and Create:

- Reflections
- Paintings
- Sketches
- Affirmations
- Songs
- Collages
- Poetry
- Questions
- Meditations
- Letters to self and others
- Stillness
- Prayers

~ Contents ~

I am	8
Grace	10
Allowing	12
Abundance	14
Knowing	16
Joy	18
Connection	20
Relationship	22
Service	24
Harmony	26
Gratitude	28
Awareness	30
Trust	32
Freedom	34
Love	36
Blessings	38
Balance	40
Openness	42
Wholeness	44
Strength	46
Patience	48
Kindness	50
Wisdom	52
Worthiness	54
Truth	56
Creativity	58
Courage	60
Giving	62
Compassion	64
Divinity	66
Presence	68
Faith	70
Forgiveness	72
Peace	74
Play	76

~~~~~~~~~~~~~~~

Remember
I am

- God is Love. I am made in the image of God. So, I am Love.
- "I am" is a declaration of my true identity and worth.

"God is Love." - I John 4:16

"So God created man in his own image, …male and female he created them." - Genesis 1:27

"Some day, after we have mastered the winds, the waves, the tides, and gravity, we shall harness the energies of LOVE. Then, for a second time in the history of the world, man will have discovered fire." - Pierre Teilhard de Chardin

Remember

Grace

- ~ I am accepted and embraced by unconditional, unlimited love--- Grace.
- ~ I am graceful.

"The entire air that surrounds me is an ocean of God, and it fills me inside and outside. I live and move and have my being in this ocean of God - in this sea of love and wisdom. God's grace is my sufficiency in all things—today, tomorrow, and a thousand years from now." - Joel Goldsmith

"Amazing grace, how sweet the sound." - John Newton

Remember
Allowing

- ~ I choose to forget myself…my stories, my worries, my fears. I lose myself in the certain, sufficient graceful fullness of Spirit.
- ~ I am surrendered. I trust the rhythms and synchronicity of Life.
- ~ I am present. I experience and trust the power of NOW.

"…convert the body into a luminous fluidity, surrendering it to the inspiration of the soul." — Isadora Duncan

"Let the peace of Christ rule in your hearts, since as members of one body you were called to peace." — Colossians 3:15

Remember
Abundance

- I am infinite, all powerful, loving Spirit Energy.
- I am abundance expressing in all ways; it flows into my life easily and effortlessly, according to the Divine plan.
- There is more than enough.

"It's the good pleasure of the Father to give you all the riches of the Kingdom." - Luke 12:32

"The Lord will grant you abundant prosperity." - Deuteronomy 28:11

"Consider how the lilies grow. They do not labor or spin. If that is how God clothes the grass of the field…how much more will he clothe you?" - Luke 12:27

Remember
Knowing

- ~ I am expansive wisdom and boundless possibility. I choose to know myself as these things always.
- ~ I take time to be still to hear the voice of Spirit within me. And…I speak only the language of this spiritual truth in my life.

"Be still and know…" — Psalm 46:10

"I have a faith, a conviction, an assurance that cannot be moved, for I am established in a love that envelops everything I contact and every person I meet." — Ernest Holmes

Remember
Joy

~ I am joyful. I choose happiness.

~ I express joy… Hallelujah!!

"Laughter is the Holy Spirit. Be the holy fool!"   - Anne Lamonte

"Happiness is when what you think, what you say, and what you do are in harmony."   - Mahatma Ghandi

Remember
Connection

~ I love all that is, for I am all that is. I constantly sense my oneness with humanity, earth and universe.

~ I am never alone. My spirit guides, angels and ancestors are with me to support, protect and guide me.

"When we look deep into the heart of a flower, we see clouds, sunshine, minerals, time, the earth and everything else in the cosmos in it. Without clouds there could be no rain, and there would be no flower."
— Thich Nhat Hanh

"Life is a closed system. What affects me, affects you."
— Avatar Training

"It's not uniformity, but a kind of unity that makes it possible for us to make an impact."
— Dorothy Height

Remember
Relationship

- Relationship is everything. People, life situations, life dramas, life challenges…happy or sad, are purposeful. These experiences help me grow and mature spiritually by providing opportunities to show forth God's grace, wisdom, peace and love.
- I have deep, joyful and fulfilling relationships.

"All persons are caught in an inescapable network of mutuality, tied in a single garment of destiny. I can never be what I ought to be until you are what you ought to be."
- Martin Luther King, Jr.

"Spiritual practice is really about weaving a network of good relationships."
- Dhyani Ywahoo

Remember

Service

- My life is purposeful. I was born into this life for a reason. There is something for each of us to do that will contribute to humanity and bring joy! Through growing and developing my inner self, I remember my purpose.

- I am a clear and willing channel of healing energy.

"I serve Jesus in all of His distressing disguises."   - Mother Teresa

"We are not seeking to escape the world, we are seeking to transform it."   - Reb Yerachmiel Ben Yisreal

"After all this time, the sun never says to the earth, 'You owe me.'"   - Anonymous

Remember
Harmony

- ~ I choose peace and harmony. I radiate loving, healing energy from within, sending it throughout the world and the universe.

- ~ I accept ALL and choose the best in every moment.

"At the heart of each of us, whatever our imperfections, there exists a silent pulse of perfect rhythm."   - George Leonard

"May it be my custom to go outdoors each day among the trees and grasses, among all growing things and there may I be alone, and enter into prayer to talk with the One that I belong to."   - Rabbi Nachman of Bratzlar

Remember
Gratitude

- ~ I am grateful for all things…the big and the small. As I open to gratitude, I attract more and more good into my life.
- ~ I give thanks for all that is manifesting in my life.
- ~ I am prosperous.

"Gratitude is knowing that what we already have is more than enough." -Anonymous

"Give thanks in all circumstances."   - I Thessalonians 5:18

"As we express our gratitude, we must never forget that the highest appreciation is not to utter words, but to live by them."
- John F. Kennedy

Remember
Awareness

- ~ I smile in the face of the ego's illusions.
- ~ I have a constant, conscious awareness of my oneness with God.
- ~ I don't have to "work" on myself. This makes me tired. I simply have to "notice" my thoughts and feelings. When I notice, I have actually become the "witness" which is the Godly presence within me!

"Beginning the day, I see that life is a miracle. Attentive to each moment, I keep my mind clear like a calm river."
- Thich Nhat Hanh

"The Spirit itself bears witness with our spirit that we are the children of God."
- Romans 8:16

Remember
Trust

- ~ I trust in the Presence of God within me. When I consciously connect to the Kingdom within, I have access to all the "riches". Trusting in myself is trusting in the Wisdom of God within me.
- ~ God is the only Presence and Power orchestrating everything, so everything works together for my highest good.
- ~ I recognize the seeming disharmonies of life as opportunities to know the Truth.

"The kingdom of heaven is within. Seek it first"
- Jesus, Luke 17:21

"I trust in you, O Lord; I say, 'You are my God.' My times are in your hands."
- Psalm 31:14-15

Remember
Freedom

- ~ I choose to be and act liberated. My spirit dances in ecstasy to the rhythm of life and soars above the clouds.
- ~ I love myself enough to accept the peace of God. I release all negativity and fear and all those who have hurt me. I am free!

"The winds of grace are always blowing…It's up to us to raise our sails."
- Deepak Chopra

"Where the Spirit of the Lord is, there is liberty."
- II Corinthians 3:7

"Free at last, free at last! Thank God Almighty, I'm free at last!"
- Martin Luther King, Jr.

Remember
Love

- ~ I accept God's gift of love and now commit to express it fully.
- ~ The love of God within works unhindered through me. I am an instrument of God's wisdom and love and I am a blessing.
- ~ I am made in the likeness and image of God. Therefore, I am Love---a deep, infinite, consistent, unconditional Love.

"God is Love." — I John 4:16

"Love heals." — Bernie Siegel

"If for every time I loved you, words could disappear. Then silence, oh, yes, silence, would be all that you could hear."
— Emily Matthews

"Love doesn't make the world go 'round.' Love is what makes the ride worthwhile."
— Franklin P. Jones

Remember
Blessings

~ I surround myself with light today. Only unconditional love may pass through this light. I love myself and others without fear.

~ I acknowledge the constant stream of good that flows into my life - I count my blessings.

"For great is your love toward me." - Psalm 86:13

"Just to be is a blessing. Just to live is holy."
- Rabbi Abraham Herschel

"And God is able to make all grace abound toward you."
- II Corinthians 9:8

Remember
Balance

~ I am whole, complete and balanced. I choose to fully enjoy earthly life, while realizing that I need nothing. I manage well the polarities of life.

"Balance means responding to criticism and to applause in the same ways---not being controlled by either."
- The Baal Shem Tov

"For everything there is a season, and a time to every purpose under the heaven."
- Ecclesiastes 3:1

Remember

Openness

- ~ I move beyond what my five senses are telling me and use my God-given spiritual senses. I am totally open to the gifts of peace, harmony, wisdom, joy and abundance. I go about my day and night relaxed---answers come.
- ~ I am open to new possibilities. I dwell in creative consciousness.

"…I create new heavens and a new earth." - Isaiah 65:17

"The human consciousness may prove the most inspiring frontier in our history, an endless wellspring of knowledge, and our means of liberation from all limitation." - Tarthang Tulku

Wholeness

- I am a perfect idea in the mind of God. It is well with me. I am as God created me.
- I am whole, healthy and peaceful in every way.

"There is in all visible things…a hidden wholeness."
- Thomas Merton

"To embrace all things means that one rids oneself of any concept of separation: male and female, self and other, life and death. Division is contrary to the nature of Tao."
- Lao Tzu

Remember

Strength

- ~ God is all there is: an infinite, all-powerful, loving Spirit Energy. My strength comes from the flow of Spirit moving in, through and around me.
- ~ When I feel fear, doubt, confusion, anger, or any kind of negativity, I acknowledge that it has no real power. Having no real power means that it is an illusion---a case of mistaken identity. I quickly acknowledge that God is the only Presence and Power, and that God is Love.

"There is a light in this world, a healing spirit more powerful than any darkness we may encounter."   - Mother Teresa

"I am the master of my fate; I am the captain of my soul."
      - William Ernest Henley

Remember
Patience

- ~ I am still and quiet periodically during my day to connect with the Source, God, my Higher Self.
- ~ Everything is working perfectly in Divine order for my highest good.
- ~ I pause to reflect before acting.

"Everything comes gradually and at its appointed hour." - Ovid

"Don't just do something, sit there!" - Anne Lamont

"Love is patient..." - I Corinthians 13: 8

Remember
Kindness

~ I practice empathy, flexibility and goodwill. I am respectful, gentle and understanding with myself and others.

"My religion is kindness." — Dalai Lama

"A smile can change the situation of the world."
— Thich Nhat Hanh

"Accept one another, just as Christ accepted you."
— Romans 15:7

Remember
Wisdom

~ I place my attention on those things and ideas that I intend to grow in others and in my life. My wisdom teaches me that whatever I give attention to will become stronger.

~ I develop my inner self first. All other things are added---they just seem to magically fall into place.

"If any of you lacks wisdom, he should ask God, who gives generously to all without finding fault." - James 1:15

"There comes a time in the spiritual journey when you start making choices from a very different place…and if a choice lines up so that it supports truth, health, happiness, wisdom, and love, it's the right choice." - Angeles Arrien

"It is the province of knowledge to speak, and it is the privilege of wisdom to listen." - Oliver Wendell Holmes

Remember
Worthiness

~ I am good at the core because I am created this way! I deserve all the good that Spirit has for me.

~ My mind, my body, my emotions and my spirit are radiant, perfect reflections of the Spirit of God.

~ All is well with me. I am a perfect idea in the mind of God. I am an individualized expression of God's perfect idea.

"I am created perfectly…in the likeness and image of God."
- Genesis 1:27

"Spirit is an invisible force made visible in all life."
- Maya Angelou

Remember
Truth

~ I own my spiritual senses which allow me to sense and speak the Truth.

~ I am impeccable with my word, speaking only those things that resonate with the highest vibrations of Love.

"You shall know the Truth and the Truth will make you free."
- John 8:32

"Speak with integrity. Say only what you mean. Avoid using the word against yourself or to gossip about others. Use the power of your word in the direction of truth and love."
- Don Miguel Ruiz

Remember
Creativity

- ~ I dwell in creative consciousness where oneness exists, where the power of my intention and my word are supreme.
- ~ I create a life of harmony, wholeness, abundance, wisdom, compassion, joy and light.
- ~ I allow the Spirit of God to express me more and more each day.
- ~ I act... boldly creating my dreams!

"There is a vitality, a life force, an energy that is translated through you into action, and because there is only one of you in all time, this expression is unique. And if you block it, it will never exist through another medium and will be lost."
- Martha Graham

Until you let the bird out of the cage, it never knows what kind of flier it's going to be."
- Ruby Dee

Remember
Courage

~ I lovingly transcend and move beyond the ego's fear by realizing the Truth. There is no real power in fear except that which I allow. I return my attention to Love which never fails.

~ I speak my Truth in wisdom and courage.

"As we are liberated from our fear, our presence automatically liberates others." — Marianne Williamson

"Dream no small dreams for they have no power." — Goethe

"Perfect Love cast out all fear." — I John 4:18

"God has not given us a spirit of fear, but of power and of love and of a sound mind." — II Timothy 1: 7

Remember
Giving

- ~ I share freely my internal and external resources with myself and with others!
- ~ I give without expectation and receive with gratitude.

"Love your neighbor as yourself."   - Leviticus 19:18

"… the spirit will emerge through the lives of ordinary people who hear a call and answer in extraordinary ways."
            - Mother Teresa

"Every good and perfect gift is from above."   - James 1:17

Remember
Compassion

~ I hold a loving consciousness toward all beings.

~ I look softly and compassionately into my own eyes.

"Compassion is by nature, peaceful and gentle, but it is also very powerful." — Dalai Lama

"Love for a person permits him to unfold, to open up, to drop his defenses, to let himself be naked not only physically but psychologically and spiritually as well." — Abraham Maslow

"To the degree that we look clearly and compassionately at ourselves, we feel confident and fearless about looking into someone else's eyes." — Unknown

Remember
Divinity

- ~ I am an expression of the fullness of God in each moment.
- ~ I am alive in God and God is alive in me- I am Divine.
- ~ My mind, body, emotions and spirit are one with the Supreme Being- God.
- ~ God is Love… a deep, infinite, consistent, unconditional Love. I don't have to do anything to earn this Love. It flows freely - it is a gift called Grace!

"We know we live in Him, and Him in us because He has given us of His Spirit."
- I John 4:13

" Spirit is an invisible force made visible in all life."
- Maya Angelou

"The same stream of Life that runs through the world runs through my veins night and day and dances in rhythmic measure."
- Rabindranath Tagore

Remember

Presence

~ There is only one Presence and one Power and it is All Good, it is All God. I acknowledge only this Presence this entire day.

~ I am the Presence of God on earth.

"It's not about doing it; it's about being it." - Gandhi

"You are the light of the world." - Jesus

"Be lamps unto yourselves; be your own confidence. Hold to the truth within yourselves…" - Buddha

Remember
Faith

- ~ My good is guaranteed. I expect miracles.
- ~ I am not my outer circumstances. I have the courage, wisdom, patience and power to change any aspect of my life to balance, abundance and harmony.

"Faith is the opening of all sides and every level of one's life to the Divine in-flow." - Martin Luther King, Jr.

"… you do not have to know how this will happen. You only have to know that it will happen." - Jack Boland

Remember
Forgiveness

~ I am forgiving. Each moment is fresh and brings new possibilities.

~ I release all negativity, resentment and past hurts.

"Where there is forgiveness there is God himself."   - Sikhism

"An attitude of forgiveness fosters channels of love and understanding in the heart."   - Jeffrey Moses

Remember

Peace

- ~ I accept the gift of a peaceful, sound mind. God is the Source of all there is, and there can be no negativity in the Presence of God. Therefore, conflict and struggle are illusions- products of a fearful ego and an unsettled mind.
- ~ I am peaceful no matter what appears to be happening.
- ~ I choose to co-create peace on earth.
- ~ Today, I am at peace. I trust the stillness within me. Every time I feel this stillness, even for a second… I smile!

"A heart at peace gives life to the body." - Proverbs 14:30

"Peace cannot be brought about by signatures on papers. When people live in the awareness that there is a close kinship between all individuals and nations, peace is the natural result."
 - Jeffrey Moses

Remember
Play

~ I attune myself with the playful rhythms of life.
~ I attract joyful, healthy, stimulating playmates and play dates.
~ I honor my Inner Child.
~ Today I lighten up!
~ I smile, laugh, giggle, chuckle, snicker or howl with glee- everyday!

"In thy presence is the fullness of joy; at thy right hand there are pleasures for evermore."   - Psalm 16:11

"I hope you'll dance."   - Tia Sillers

"Play is the only way the highest intelligence of humankind can unfold."   - Joseph Chilton Pearce

About the Author
Carolyn M. McKanders

A Joyful Servant, Spiritual Teacher and Counselor

Spiritual teaching and counseling are experiences that help us to discover the Truth about ourselves; they enable us to understand and feel our spiritual identity - one of love, beauty and wholeness. These experiences help us to ask and answer some of life's most challenging questions about which we often wonder. They teach us that our resources are God-given and mainly internal and seek to connect us to these resources- returning us to Love. Knowing who we are grounds us and brings peace and balance, enabling us to heal more quickly, forgive more readily, and love ourselves and others more completely. *And the Truth shall make you free* (John 8:32). Carolyn counsels, teaches and facilitates spiritual retreats.

Educational Consultant

Carolyn McKanders is an international educational consultant specializing in individual, group and organizational development. Carolyn's passion is promoting quality human relationships through communication, collaboration, and leadership skills development. Over the past five years she has worked as an independent consultant providing staff development through presentations, group facilitation, and instructional and leadership coaching. Her expertise includes providing polarity management training that helps organizations identify and manage competing tensions inherent in social systems. Carolyn's background includes 28 years of experience in Detroit Public Schools as a teacher, counselor and staff development specialist.

Carolyn earned a Bachelor of Science degree in Child Development and Education from Michigan State University; a Master of Arts in Counseling and Education from the University of Michigan; and a Master of Social Work degree in Family and Child Services from Eastern Michigan University.

She is blessed with a loving, supportive husband, Kenneth McKanders, J.D. and four phenomenal children: Kimberly McKanders, M.D., Karla McKanders, J.D., Kristal McKanders, M.A. and Kenny, a high school senior.

Carolyn expresses gratitude to God, the Source of all and within all. Her wish is to express love, peace and wisdom fully as a joyful servant!

To contact Carolyn McKanders or for more information:

Carolyn McKanders, MSW
c/o PriorityONE Publications
P.O. Box 725 • Farmington, MI 48332
cmckanders@p1pubs.com
(313) 378-5078

www.ingramcontent.com/pod-product-compliance
Lightning Source LLC
Chambersburg PA
CBHW051421070526
44584CB00023B/3532